SCIEN[illegible]GIC

CONTENTS

Written by Marjorie Newman
Illustrated by Margaret Clark-Jones

Collins Educational
An imprint of HarperCollins*Publishers*

Introduction

Here are some magic tricks for you to try out on your friends. Unless you know something about science, these tricks can seem like magic.

Of course, just doing the tricks won't make you a magician. It's the *way* you do them. Practise until you can do the tricks easily. Then think about what you will say when you perform them. You could make up a story to fit a trick, or tell jokes during the trick.

You could also pretend to have made a mistake. Then perform the trick properly. Be prepared in case you do make a mistake!

Make your performance different from anyone else's. Work out a show, including several tricks. Keep it short – fifteen minutes is about the right length. Start with a good trick, and end with your best one.

Have fun!

Before You Start

PREPARE YOUR MAGIC TABLE AND CLOTH

You will need a table which gives you room to perform your tricks.

Spread your magic cloth over it. You may be able to find a brightly patterned table cloth. Or draw some magic patterns on a large piece of white paper.

Cover your cloth with clear polythene or plastic. This will protect the cloth, especially when you are using water.

MAKE YOUR COSTUME

Ask an adult for some material for a magic cloak. Fasten it on.

Remember you need your hands free.

You can make a pointed hat from paper or card:

MAKE YOUR MAGIC WAND

Find a stick of the right length. (A piece of dowel rod is very good.)

Paint it black, with white ends.

GET YOUR AUDIENCE TOGETHER

It's better to start with a small audience of one, two or three people.

You could include adults in your audience – especially if it's a long time since they did any science!

Your audience may sit facing you or they may stand round the table. It depends on the trick.

The Heavy Paper

YOU WILL NEED:

- four plain pieces of paper of roughly the same size and weight

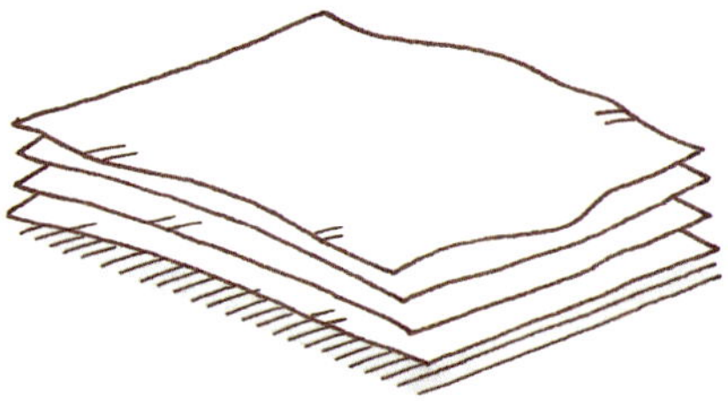

GETTING READY

1 On one piece of paper draw something heavy, like a brick.
2 On another piece draw something light, like a feather.
3 Keep the other two pieces of paper plain.

TO PERFORM THE TRICK

1 Tell your audience that you have magic powers that can make paper heavy.

2 Hold the two plain pieces up at arm's length.

3 Let go of them and show your audience that the two pieces reach the ground at about the same time.

4 Now bring forward your drawings. Wave your magic wand over them. Say that when you drop them now, the 'heavy' one will reach the ground first. The audience will not believe you.

5 Pick up the 'heavy' piece of paper and crumple it up into a ball.

6 Hold up both drawings and let them go at the same time. The crumpled one will certainly reach the ground first!

WHY DOES THIS WORK?

If you hold the crumpled ball and the flat square under a light you will see their shadows on the floor. The shadow shows you clearly which of the pieces of paper will have more air caught under it when you drop them. The greater the amount of air to hold it up, the slower the paper will fall.

Keeping the Paper Dry

YOU WILL NEED:

- a glass jug full of water
- a piece of paper
- a drinking glass

TO PERFORM THE TRICK

1 Tell your audience you can keep a piece of paper dry under water.

2 Crumple up the paper.

3 Push it well down into the bottom of the glass. Wave your magic wand and say, "Bam Boozalam".

4 Now turn the glass upside down and push it, rim first, into the jug of water. Try not to tilt the glass.

5 The paper will stay dry.

WHY DOES THIS WORK?

It works because there is air trapped in the glass, stopping water from reaching the paper – this air pushes the water back.

You can feel how strong the **buoyancy** of the trapped air is while you are trying to push the glass into the water.

For Fun – The Two Glasses Trick

YOU WILL NEED:

- a large jug of water
- two drinking glasses

TO PERFORM THE TRICK

1 Tell your audience you can fill the glasses with water from the jug, yet the jug will still have the same amount of water in it.

2 Then put the two glasses into the jug of water. Abracadabra!

Blow!

You will need:

- a 250ml plastic bottle
- a scrap of newspaper about 5cm by 4cm

To perform the trick

1 Put the bottle on its side with its mouth at the edge of the table.

2 Crumple up the newspaper into a ball and put it just inside the mouth of the bottle. You will need to hold the bottle steady.

3 Ask someone in your audience to try to blow the paper right down to the end of the bottle. To give them the *wrong* idea, take a deep breath and give a quick, hard puff towards your audience.

4 The audience will think this is easy. Two or three people may want a turn.
But the harder they puff, the more the paper will pop out of the bottle.

5 When your audience is puffed out, wave your wand over the bottle, saying the magic words, "Sim Sala Bim".

6 Now blow steadily and gently towards the bottom of the mouth of the bottle.

7 The paper will go right into the bottle.

WHY DOES THIS WORK?

When you give a quick, hard puff, the air already in the bottle doesn't have time to get out of the way – see **(a)**. So when you finish blowing, the air all comes rushing out again, bringing the ball of paper with it – see **(b)**.

When you blow gently in at the bottom of the mouth of the bottle, the air has time to come out at the top – see **(c)**.

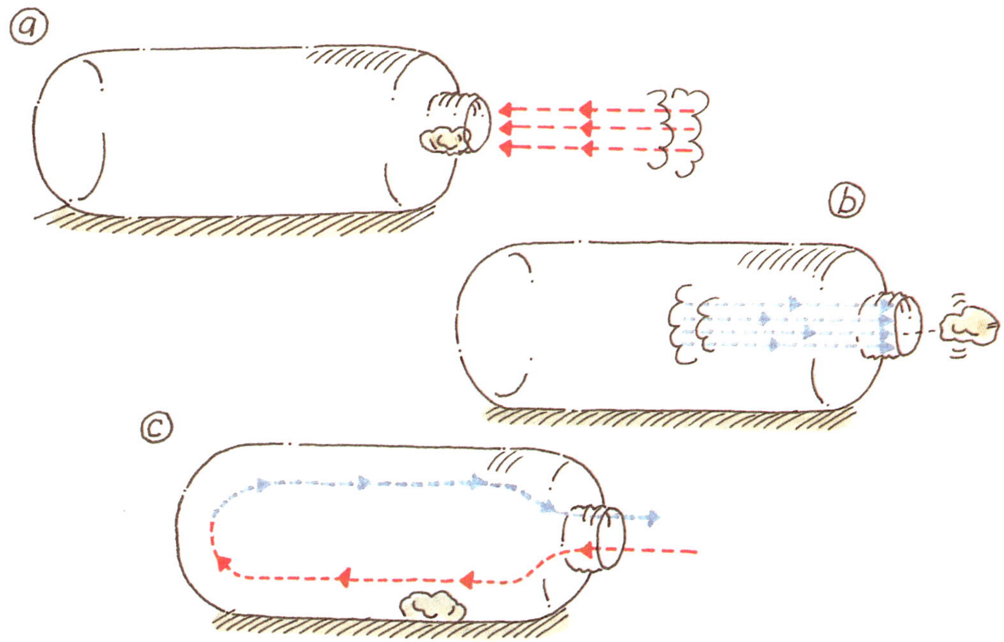

Get the Coin Into the Bottle

YOU WILL NEED:

- a five pence piece
- a milk bottle
- a used wooden matchstick

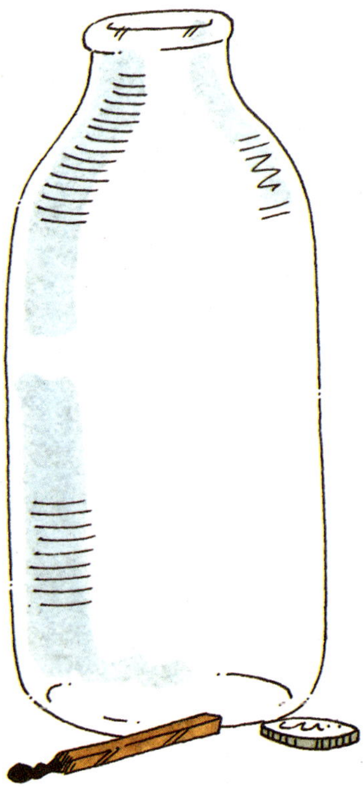

TO PERFORM THE TRICK

1 Carefully make the matchstick into a V shape. The wood will split, but do not break it right through.

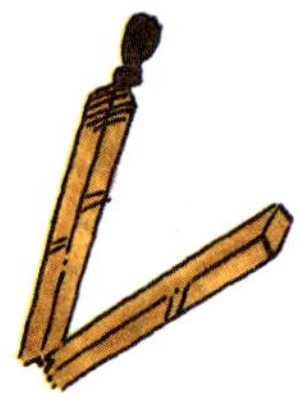

2 Lay the stick across the top of the bottle. Then carefully balance the five pence piece on the bent stick. Remember to practise first.

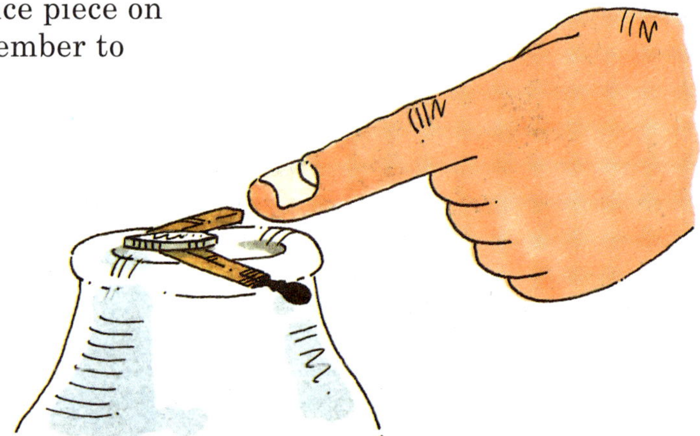

3 Tell your audience you can make the five pence piece drop into the bottle without touching the stick, or taking the stick away.

4 Drip water onto the stick where it is bent.

5 The stick will gradually straighten out.

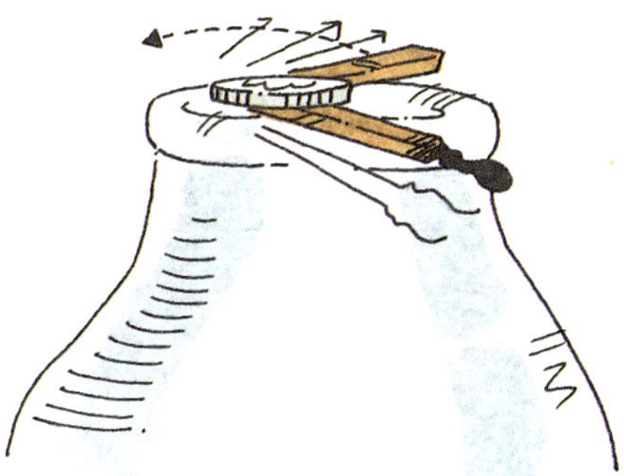

6 The coin should fall down into the bottle.

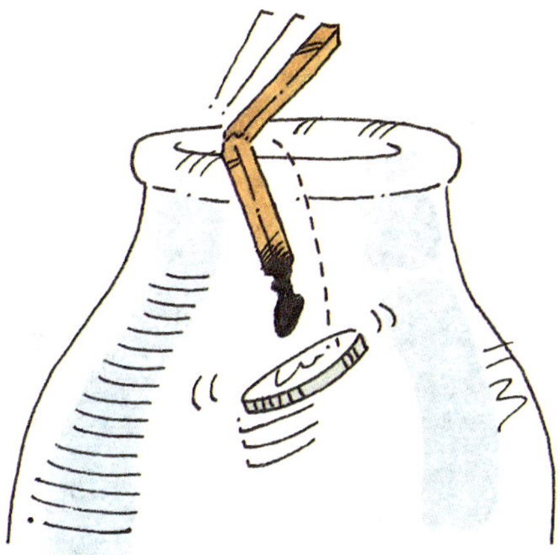

Why does this work?

It works because wood is made of **wood fibres** – see **(a)**.

Dampness makes the fibres swell, and so straighten out. This unbalances the coin – see **(b)**.

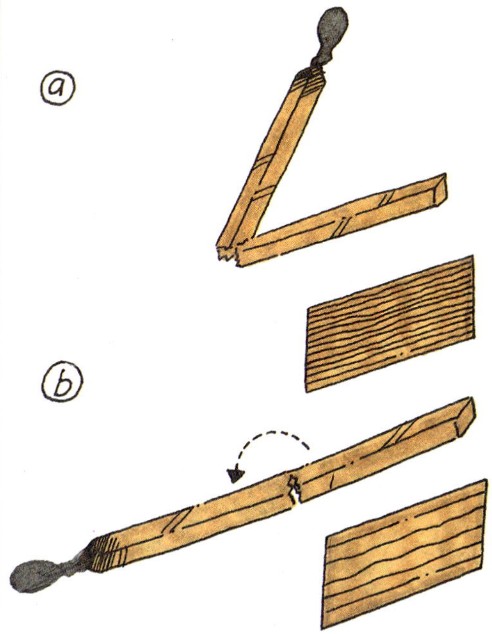

The Amazingly Strong Cotton Thread

YOU WILL NEED:

- a house brick
- two pieces of cotton thread
- a bowl of water

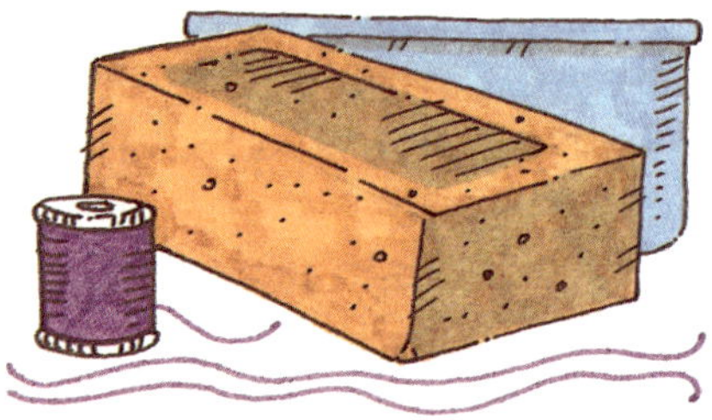

GETTING READY

Experiment with different threads to find one of the right strength. You need a thread which is strong enough to lift the brick in water, but not strong enough to lift the brick in air.

TO PERFORM THE TRICK

1 Have the bowl of water handy. Let the audience stand round. Show them the brick and a piece of thread.

2 Tie the cotton thread round the brick.

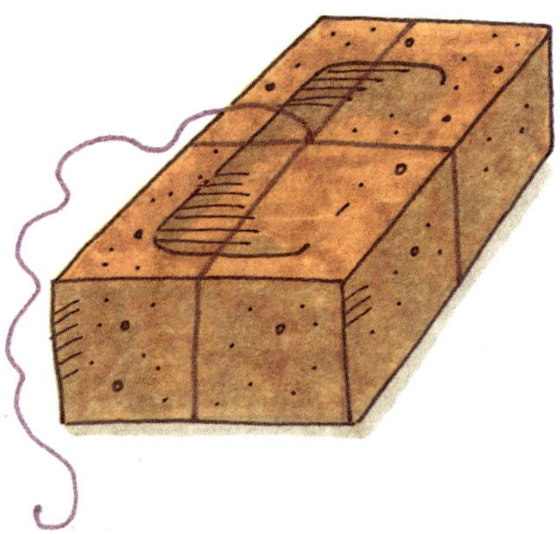

3 Say that with your amazing powers, you can pick up the brick by the piece of thread.

4 Let one of the audience try. The thread will break. You will need your second piece.

5 Put the brick into the water by hand. Do not lower it in by the thread – it will break. Wave your magic wand. As you lift the brick by the thread, pretend it is still very heavy. But Hey Presto! You can do it!

WHY DOES THIS WORK?

It works because the brick pushes the water out of the way. (You will see the water rise in the bowl as you put the brick in.) The water will try to get back to its original space, pushing the brick upwards and so the brick seems to be lighter. If you try to lift the brick out of the water, the water can go back to where it was before and stops pushing at the brick. The thread will then break.

Water pushing the brick upwards

Yellow, Brown and Bubbly White

YOU WILL NEED:

- vinegar
- cooking oil
- two clear 250ml plastic bottles

GETTING READY

1 Take the labels off the clear bottles.

2 Pour some vinegar into one bottle.

3 Pour about the same amount of oil into the other. Put the tops back on to guard against spills.

4 It's a good idea to give the liquids new names. (You could then re-name the trick.)

5 Never tell the audience what is really in the bottles. And make sure no-one comes near enough to smell the vinegar!

TO PERFORM THE TRICK

1 Show the two bottles to your audience and tell them that you can have the brown and yellow liquids in the same bottle without them getting mixed up. Now wave your magic wand.

2 Take off the bottle tops. Holding both bottles, very gently trickle the oil down onto the vinegar. The oil will float on top.

3 Show the audience the bottle. When they finish clapping, say you will now make the yellow turn bubbly white.

4 Put the top back on. Wave your magic wand over the bottle. Then pick the bottle up and shake it well. The contents will go bubbly white.

5 Stand the bottle on the table to let the mixture settle. Perhaps tell a joke to keep the attention of the audience while you are waiting. Soon you will notice the two liquids separating. Ali Kassim! Only the top layer will be bubbly white!

WHY DOES THIS WORK?

Liquids don't all weigh the same. Oil is lighter than vinegar: it has a lower **density** so it floats on the top. When you shake the bottle, both liquids turn into tiny droplets and mix together. The layers separate again because oil will not dissolve in vinegar (or water). The oil still looks white because some of the vinegar droplets are still mixed in.

Make a Coin Disappear

YOU WILL NEED:

- a coin
- a milk bottle
- a jug of water

TO PERFORM THE TRICK

1 Let your audience stand round. Tell them that, with your magic powers, you can make a coin disappear.

2 Put the coin on the table and stand the empty milk bottle on the coin.

3 Tell your audience to look at the coin through the side of the milk bottle. It is easy to see the coin.

4 Now tell them to move away from the table by one metre. They can still see the coin.

5 Tell your audience to stay there, watching the coin.

6 Now pour water from the jug into the bottle, saying, "Now you see it, now you don't!"

7 Your audience will see the coin disappear.

WHY DOES THIS WORK?

Usually we can see things because light beams travel from the sun – or from any other light source – and hit the object. These beams then bounce straight off the object to our eyes. The beams are travelling through air. This is what our eyes are used to when they judge distance – see **(a)**.

But as the beam passes from water to air, it bends. This is called **refraction**. In this trick because the light is bent, our eyes see right over the top of the coin to the other side of the bottle – see **(b)**.

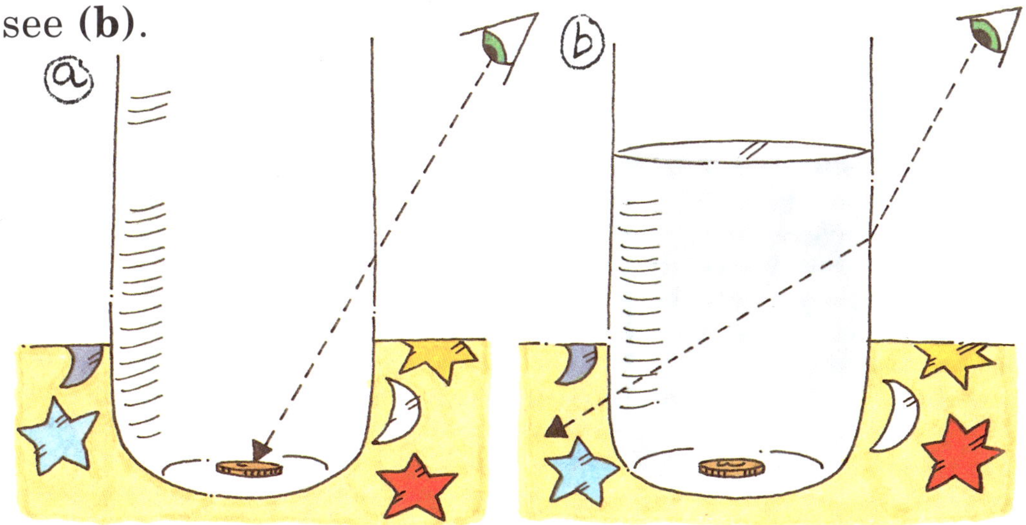

The Floating Coin

Here are some more tricks which work because our eyes are used to looking through air, not water. Try these just for yourself.

You will need:

- a coin
- a clear bowl half full of water

To perform the trick

1 Put the coin in the water.

2 When you look at the coin from above, you can see it lying on the bottom of the bowl.

3 Now look through the side of the bowl. The coin looks as though it is floating at the top of the water.

The Bent Pencil

YOU WILL NEED:

- a pencil
- a glass full of water

TO PERFORM THE TRICK

1 Put the pencil into the water.

2 Lift the glass up to your eye level.

3 The pencil will look bent.

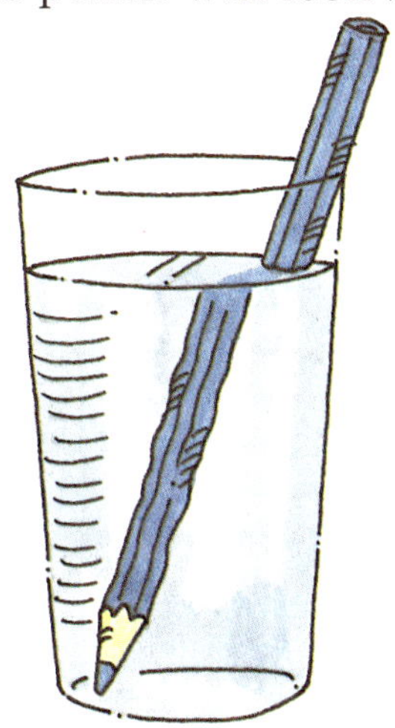

Look at a swimming pool filled with water.

The bottom will look much closer than it really is, so the pool appears shallower.

If you look down at your legs in the swimming pool, they will seem shorter than they really are.

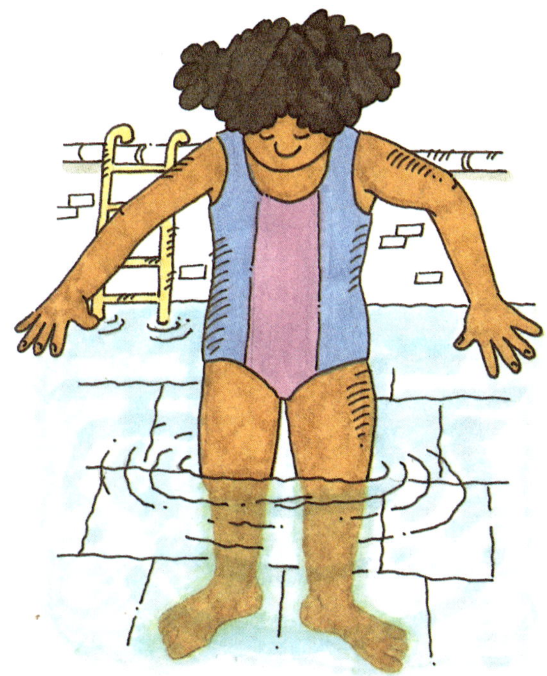

The Bouncing Hat

You will need:

- a hat
- an elastic band
- two safety pins

Getting Ready

Pin the elastic band across the inside of the hat, at the bottom.

The elastic band should not be too long. You will need to experiment a bit.

To perform the trick

1 Tell your audience that you can make the hat bounce up. Say, "This is a magic hat. It doesn't like staying on my head."

2 Put the hat on.

3 Pull it down.

4 Then let it go.

5 The hat will bounce up.

WHY DOES THIS WORK?

It works because rubber bands like to be as short as possible.

Stretching them builds up **energy** in them. As soon as you let them go they will use this energy to unstretch themselves, and the hat will rise.

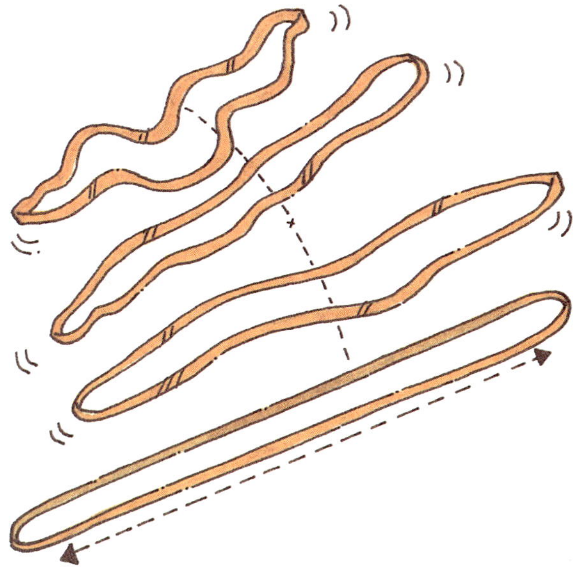

Call That Coin!

YOU WILL NEED:

- two large coins
- one small coin
- a drinking glass

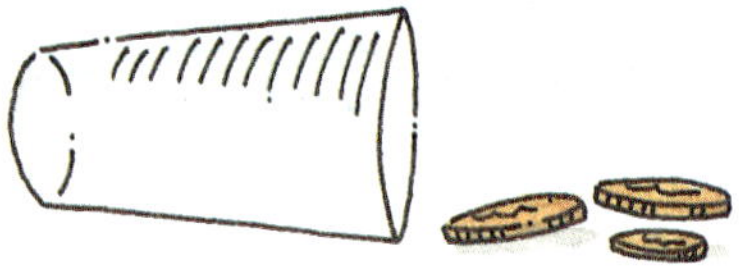

GETTING READY:

This trick only works on a piece of material. A tablecloth is fine, but any stretchy material will do as long as you lay it flat and hold it steady behind the glass with one hand. Or you could ask an assistant from your audience to hold it steady.

TO PERFORM THE TRICK

1 Arrange the coins in a row on the cloth. The small coin must be in the middle.

2 Turn the glass upside down, and rest it on the two large coins. The small coin is now under the glass.

3 Tell your audience you can make the small coin come out without anyone touching the glass or any of the coins. Wave your magic wand over the glass.

4 Then scratch the cloth with one finger 3 or 4cm in front of the glass. Say, "Come out, coin! Come out, coin!" Keep scratching, and the coin will start to 'walk' towards your finger.

5 If you have an eager audience, you could ask them to join in, chanting, "Come out, coin! Come out, coin!" until you hold up the coin and shout, "Hey Presto!"

WHY DOES THIS WORK?

This trick works because material is a bit like the elastic rubber band. When you scratch the material with your fingernail you stretch it a little bit, and the coin moves forward on it.

Every time you lift your fingernail the material springs back into its first shape. The material slides back under the coin because the coin is too heavy to go back with it.

So with every scratch the coin moves a tiny bit forward, and stays there until the next scratch.

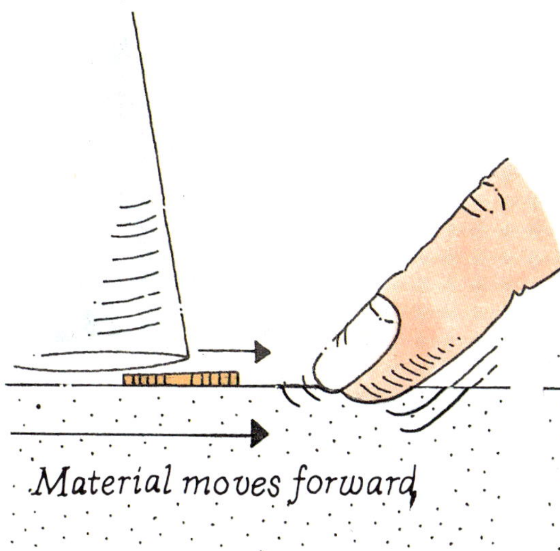

Glossary

buoyancy
the ability to float in a liquid or to rise in a liquid, air or other gas

density
how much something weighs for its size. Everything – including air and water – is made up of tiny pieces or particles, that are too small to see. If an object has high density, the particles are packed very tightly together. If an object has low density, the particles are very loosely connected.

energy
the strength or power that people or objects have to do work. It is also the power from various sources such as coal or electricity which makes other things work.

refraction
the bending of light as light beams travel through different things, such as air, water or glass

wood fibres
fine threads of wood which are joined together and make a whole piece of wood